BACKYARD CHICKENS

THE ULTIMATE BEGINNERS GUIDE TO CHOOSING A BREED, CHICKEN COOP, AND RAISING BACKYARD CHICKENS

EMILY WALSH

© 2015 by Backyard Producer Publishing

All rights reserved. No part of this publication may be reproduced, distributed, or transmitted in any form or by any means, including photocopying, recording, or other electronic or mechanical methods, without the prior written permission of the publisher, except in the case of brief quotations embodied in critical reviews and certain other noncommercial uses permitted by copyright law.

A Free Gift For You

As a thank you for purchasing this book, I want to give you a free Chicken Coop Plan PDF. With this you will easily be able to build your dream chicken coop. It comes complete with material list and step by step instructions. You can download it at BackyardProducer.com/Chicken-Coop-PDF.

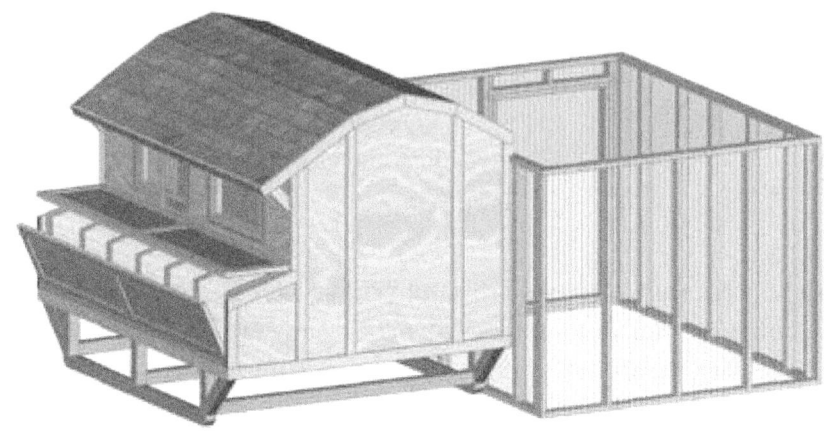

Why I Wrote This Book

So many of us have become disconnected from our food supply. We have no idea where our food comes from or what actually goes into it. It just magically appears on the supermarket shelves and eventually into our cupboards and our refrigerators. Many of us actually want it this way. We don't want to have to think about the living conditions of the animals we eat or their byproducts. It's easier to just imagine that our food magically appears in their packages and cartons.

I was one of these people. It was easier to just go to the store and grab a carton of eggs without wondering if the chicken was fed a proper diet. I didn't have to wonder if it was allowed outside to peck and scratch like a chicken should.

This all changed when I became a mother. I was suddenly concerned with what was going into my children's bodies even though I dismissed those same thoughts when it came to my own body years before. I began looking for healthier foods and also in the process of looking at where our food actually comes from.

It was during this process that I stumbled upon backyard chickens and it seemed like the perfect fit. I could provide eggs and occasionally meat onto our family table while knowing what went into the chickens and where our food came from. That was 7 years ago and this book describes some of the things that I have learned in that time.

I hope you enjoy and thank you for purchasing my book!

TABLE OF CONTENTS

A Free Gift For You

Why I Wrote This Book

TABLE OF CONTENTS

Introduction

Why You Should Consider Raising Chickens?

Is Raising Chickens Compatible With Your Lifestyle?

Required Investment

Building a Coop

Breeds to consider

Living Conditions of Your Chickens

Feeding Your Chickens

Health Concerns

How To Take Care of a Chick

Pecking Order

Dealing with Predators

Conclusion

Introduction

Organic living is all the rage these days. There was a brief time in human history when the industrial revolution was at its peak. During that time, it was considered chic and modern to replace everything natural with something churned out artificially. Formula milks replaced maternal nourishment, diapers took the place of cloth, fruits were genetically engineered and even chickens were genetically modified to give higher egg and meat production. For many of us, we are still stuck in this phase.

However, many people are realizing that all the artificial and modified produce is tasteless and lacks nutrition. Genetically modified fruits are beautiful to look at but they are bland in taste. There is no richness of flavor that can make you squirm with delight as you take a bite of a juicy mango.

Hence it is only natural that people are starting to return towards the more natural way of living. The kind of lifestyle that shuns consumerism and supports self-sustained living. Today many people maintain a small kitchen garden where they grow their own fruits and vegetable that are enough for their small families. Unfortunately the whole system is designed to promote consumerism. It is very hard to be self-sustained. Though more and more people are making an effort to live a life that is more close to nature.

One of the many success stories of genetic modification was the introduction of broiler chickens. They grew up fast and hence were perfect for a quick but long term supply of meat. The introduction of broiler chicken made it possible for fast food chains such as McDonalds and Burger King to churn out pounds of poultry based food items.

Though broiler chickens helped fill the market gap, it is far from being the perfect source of protein. Research has shown that broiler meat is not as rich in nutrients as in other chicken meats. It also has a much higher fat content. Market bought eggs lack the taste and richness of the eggs obtained from a normal hen.

Due to these reservations, it was only natural that people try to raise their own chickens for safer and better quality eggs and meat. This might sound like an extremely tedious task but it is not as difficult as it seems. It's also quite fulfilling to know where your meat comes from.

This book has been written to help you out in your initiative to raise backyard chickens and take your first step towards sustained living. It answers all your basic questions about trying to raise your own flock of chickens in the limited space that you might have. From building a coop to hatching an egg-I have covered all the steps.

By the time you finish this book, you'll be equipped with all the vital knowledge that you need to raise your own flock of backyard chickens.

Why You Should Consider Raising Chickens?

The most obvious benefit of raising chickens is the lure of healthy meat and eggs. When you raise your own chickens you know what went into that meat. When you buy meat that has been raised and processed at a poultry farm, you can never know for sure what kind of feed was given to the chicken. There has been a controversy in the past about poultry farms feeding their chickens steroids. Consumption of that meat was causing hormonal imbalance in teens and preteens. This was a huge red flag for me. You do not want to be eating something that might have disastrous effects on your health and the health of the ones you love. Contrarily, when you raise your own chickens you know that there are no nasty chemicals involved.

Similar to meat, the kind of food that is fed to the chickens will affect the quality of the eggs. Even eggs that are marked as "organic" at your local grocers are not hundred percent natural. Unless you buy directly from a country farm, you can never be sure about the quality of the egg.

Many people complain about the bland taste of the store bought egg. Free range eggs on the other hand are smaller in size but are much more richer in taste. They are also filled with beneficial nutrients such as Vitamin A, Beta Carotene and Omega 3. Most store bought eggs on the other hand are high in cholesterol and fat content but much lower in vital minerals and vitamins.

Another point to note is that the eggs available in stores are already a few days or weeks old. The quality of the egg can deteriorate rapidly over the course of time. Especially if the weather is warm.

However if you have your own flock of chickens, you'll have an ample supply of eggs that are always fresh and taste great.

If you're someone who loves our feathered friends, then you'll definitely enjoy raising chickens. Small chicks and even full grown hens are incredibly cute (Chicken Little anyone?). They are so naive that they border on being absurd. It can be quite entertaining to watch them go about their daily business. Many people have uploaded hilarious videos of their hens on YouTube.

Have you ever seen a hen run? Especially run towards food? If you haven't then you are in for a treat. Watching them is no less amusing than watching a staged comedy show.

However do not confuse their simple mindedness with dumbness. Chickens are reasonably smart and responsive. If you give them love and food, they'll flock around you at the sight of you and peck affectionately at your feet.

You don't have to necessarily raise them as livestock. Hens can also be great pets.

If you have a small baby or a toddler then keeping a pet sometimes be risky. There is always a risk of an unintentional graze or scratch with a dog or a cat. Hens on the other hand are completely safe to be kept around your baby. Your toddler can also have some light hearted fun by chasing the hens around the yard. Chickens are gentle creatures by nature and will not flock together to harm your baby in any way. Though you should firmly explain to your child to not pull or tug at their feathers as it is a cruel thing to do.

On top of all these benefits, chickens are extremely budget friendly pets. Unlike cats and dogs, they do not require constant visits to the vet. There is also no need to spay and neuter them. Hens do not have specific food requirements and with the right planning can even be raised on leftovers. You'll be surprised to read that raising a flock of chickens is much cheaper than keeping a pair of parrots.

Is Raising Chickens Compatible With Your Lifestyle?

Before you make the decision of raising chickens in your backyard, there are a few points that you should consider. The first and foremost question you need to ask yourself is that, "Is it compatible with my lifestyle?" followed by, "Would I be able to manage it?" I have compiled a few points that will help you answer these questions.

Check in with your local law enforcement agency to inquire about the legal stance of keeping chickens. In most states, it is perfectly legal to keep and raise chickens. However the details of the laws applicable can vary from city to city. In some areas, it is prohibited to keep a rooster within the city limits. This is simply because roosters make a lot of noise and can be a cause of annoyance for you neighbors. While you're at it, it is also recommended to ask your neighbors. You are not necessarily required to ask their opinion, but it still counts as good manners to inquire in case someone in the vicinity has an allergy to certain birds.

Your next step should be to evaluate the space available to you realistically. An 8x8 sq. ft. of space is ideal for a flock of about four to five hens. However there is no hard and fast rule regarding the space that is required. It all depends upon the individual behaviors of your hens. Some are more sharing by temperament while others are relatively fussy. The amount of space required also varies from breed to breed. Some people also let their hens go free range and roam the area at will. This is the ideal situation however it can also be very dangerous in case of predators. You should have enough space that every chicken has easy access to food and water. If you plan on raising chicks, you will require more space as there is a danger of trampling in constricted spaces.

ANALYZE YOUR JOB SCHEDULE AND WORK HOURS CAREFULLY.

Do you have fixed job hours? Or do you work shifts?

Do you work a standard nine to five job?

Can you take time out for feeding the hens at a set time?

If the answer to any of these questions is "No" then you should reconsider your decision. Chickens are relatively low maintenance pets but they still require regular feeding and watering. Ideally you should feed them twice a day. Once in the early morning and once in the evening before sunset. It is advised that you keep a regular feeding schedule. If your job has no set hours, you might not be able to achieve that. Erratic schedules can confuse your hens and they might not be as happy and content as they should be. This can also lead to poor egg production.

YOUR NEXT STEP SHOULD BE TO HONESTLY ASSESS YOUR LIFESTYLE AND HABITS.

Are you a couch potato or do you enjoy outdoor activity?

If you are of the former kind, then the task might prove a little trying for you. It does not mean that you cannot raise chickens but that you'll have to put in a little more conscious effort. You cannot ignore your chickens just because your favorite television show is on air. Who knows, you might even come to enjoy spending some time outdoors.

If you're someone who really loves gardening and seeing flowers bloom, then keeping hens can be a bit of a challenge. It is possible to juggle these both hobbies side by side but it will require some extra planning. Hens will help you out by eating weeds and pests but unfortunately they cannot differentiate between weeds and saplings that you planted. They will dine on the fresh saplings the first chance they get. They might also dig out the seeds that you planted and snack on them. If you have not carefully planned this out ahead of time, it can become frustrating very quickly.

However on the upside, the problem can be managed by separating the garden area with the help of a fence. You can also keep your chickens in the coop at all times during the early spring season. Once the plants have grown and the flowers have bloomed, then your mischievous little friends will no longer pose a threat.

Required Investment

Most of the time adopting a pet is free of cost. Especially if the pet in question is a dog or a cat. However chickens are not exactly pets. They can be classified somewhere between pets and livestock. Hence keeping your own backyard chickens requires some initial investment. In retrospect the amount you will save by not buying eggs and meat, is much more than the initial investment. Also the quality of your food will increase by many folds.

The first item that requires high initial capital is a coop. Even if you plan to allow your chickens to free range, you'll still need a coop for night time. You can either buy a pre-made coop or build one yourself. Both are viable options depending upon your area and lifestyle.

Buying a pre-made chicken coop can cost you anywhere from $100 to about $1000. Prices vary according to sizes and design. Some chicken coops are elaborately designed and therefore cost more. You do not need such a fancy coop as chickens unlike parrots are indifferent to colors and designs. Choose something that is functional, airy and fits within your budget.

If you like to do things yourself, then you can build you chicken coop with tin, wooden planks and some chicken wire. However if you are a beginner, I recommend buying a pre-made chicken coop to save time and hassle.

In addition to the basic living unit, you'll also need feeding trays and watering cans. There are many different designs available and prices can range from $8 to $30. I recommend self-filling watering cans as they are easier to manage. You can also fix the feeding trays in place to prevent your hens from toppling it over. The feeding tray you choose should be long enough that all your hens can eat comfortably at one time. This will cut down on your hens fighting.

For hygienic purposes, I recommend lining the coop with wood shavings. You should avoid using straw as a base for your coop, especially if you have chicks amongst your flock. The straws can get stuck inside their wind pipe and can be fatal. Wood shavings cost about $6 per bag. Depending upon the size of your coop, you will need a few bag of those.

Once you have your coop well and ready, you need to buy chickens. This is the most important part. Do your research well and pinpoint your needs.

Are you interested in eggs?

Are you interested in meat?

Depending upon your needs, there are various breeds you can choose from. However for a beginner, the more pressing matter is the age of the chicken to purchase. Small chicks are usually cheaper but they are also more difficult to raise and take care of. Mortality rate might be high. Even if you are well versed in taking care of the chicks, you'll have to wait at least six months before they start laying eggs. There is also a chance of some of your chicks growing to be roosters instead of hens. On an average a young chick can cost you about $2 -$4.

The obvious advantage of getting a full grown flock is that they'll give you results almost immediately. However the cost is much higher. A full grown laying hen can cost you anywhere from $15 to $30. Though exact prices can vary depending upon the market situation and your location.

I recommend getting about four to six weeks old chicks if they are available in your area. They are much more stable than young chicks and do not cost as much as an adult hen. Usually the mortality in chicks occurs in the first few weeks so you can avoid this by buying slightly older chicks.

On average, setting up a flock of chickens can cost you about $300 to $400. It might seem like a lot of money but is actually very minimal in comparison to the capital cost required for keeping other livestock animals such as goats, pigs and cows. Also in the long run it will prove to be a valuable and beneficial setup for you and your family.

Building a Coop

Depending upon the area you live in, your lifestyle and financial constrains, buying a pre-made coop might not be the most viable option for you. If that's the case, you'll obviously need to build your own coop. If you choose to go down this route, you'll have two options:

1. Get pre-made frames and assemble them yourself.

This is similar to building a kids' play house. You'll have everything in the kit you buy, you'll just need to assemble them together. This is relatively easier than building from scratch.

2. Build your coop from scratch.

Alternatively you can obtain raw materials and build the coop yourself. You can decide the design and plan according to your wants and needs. This requires effective planning, a step by step approach and a set of functional tools.

If you choose the latter option, then this section will guide you on how to build your chicken coop from scratch.

Even if you have sufficient space in your backyard, you'll still need to select a dedicated area for your coop. I suggest building your coop either under the shade of a tree or adjacent to a wall. Not only will it look more beautiful, but will shield your chickens from the harsh effects of weather.

Before you begin building, you'll need to assemble a set of necessary tools required. You'll have most of these tools stowed in some part of your garage. If you do not own them, you'll either need to buy them or you can also borrow them from a friend or neighbor.

The tools you'll need are:

- Hammer
- Saw
- Drill
- Nails
- Hinges
- Workbench
- Measuring Tape
- Gloves
- Mask

Once you have assembled all the tools you'll need, you'll then need to buy the actual material. You'll need either wood planks or plywood to be used for the basic frame structure. Plywood is cheaper but it is also not as strong as wood. If you live in a windy area, than there might be a chance of the wind knocking over the plywood structure. If you can manage it financially, I suggest using wooden planks. You can get them from any hardware store in your area. I suggest buying the planks or plywood sheets in different sizes instead of one uniform size. It will save you the hassle of repeated cuttings.

Once you have acquired the material for the frame, you'll need to buy some chicken wire. This wire will go onto the windows and doors of the coop to allow ventilation. If your structure is fully closed off, your chickens won't be very happy.

Building a chicken coop is not a simple task. You cannot just assemble together the materials and start building on a whim. In some ways, it is similar to construction of a house. Only that it is a house for your hens. You'll need a proper layout and plan. For that, you can a free chicken coop plan by going to BackyardProducer.com/Chicken-Coop-PDF.

Finalize a layout that suits your needs and seems easy to construct. Keep in mind that your coop should have a cover to keep out the rain and snow if your area is prone to this type of weather. A tin or wooden roof would work well for this purpose. It is also preferable that there should be a removable curtain to cover the ventilation windows. This is especially important in case of rain and wind as hens can easily be taken ill in these weather conditions.

The entrance to the coop should be large enough to allow you to enter it without discomfort or hindrance. This is so because on a biweekly or monthly basis, you'll need to enter the coop to clean and disinfect it. You also need a reasonably sized door to conveniently retrieve eggs from the nesting area daily.

On the weekend or any other off day, begin construction of your new chicken coop. Follow the plans closely and start building the frame first. You will be installing the wire mesh later on, after the basic structure is ready. Do not try to do all at once. Seek the help of a friend or a family member. It is a long and tedious task, so be mentally prepared for the fact that it might take several days before you are finished.

Once you have completed the basic structure and are satisfied, you'll need to move on to building the accessories for your chicken coop.

Hens by nature like to sleep and rest on an elevated surface. To accommodate this habit, you'll need to install a perch. The length of the perch should be according to the number of hens that you plan on keeping. It should be long enough that hens can rest comfortably without being cramped. The perch should be made out of wood. If you can somehow manage to install a tree trunk in there, that would be ideal. Metallic perches are not comfortable for the bird as they cannot grip this material like they can wood.

In addition to the perch, you'll also need to allocate space for a dedicated nesting area. This is the place where your hens will lay eggs. You can make simple nests by filling baskets with straw. You can make this as elaborate or as simple as you want.

With time, you can add extra details such as paint and decorations that will make the coop more aesthetically pleasing. Building a custom design coop is a painstaking and wearisome task but it will be worth it in the end when your hens are safe and content within it.

BREEDS TO CONSIDER

Once you have built your coop, you just need to fill it with a flock of chickens. If you are planning on breeding, then the ideal setup should contain five hens and one rooster. However some cities do not allow you to keep roosters within the city limits because of the noise they make. This is not a big issue unless you plan on breeding. The most common misconception is that hens cannot lay eggs without a rooster. This is untrue. Your hens will lay eggs without a rooster but they will not be fertile.

As an amateur, you should keep in mind that different breeds have different kinds of temperaments. A breed with a wild and adventurous temperament would be fun to raise but it would also be more difficult. In this sense, choosing a chicken breed is really similar to choosing a dog breed. For example, a Pug is much easier to raise than a Doberman pinscher as a Pug has a more relaxed and easy outlook of life. It does not mean that you cannot keep a more spirited breed, but just that it will require a little more effort.

However just like all animals, the breed can only give you a general idea about what to expect. The nature and temperament can vary from hen to hen even within the same breed.

The second point to consider before choosing a breed is your set of needs. If you're raising chickens for eggs, the recommended breeds would be different than if you're more interested in meat. If you seek to keep your flock as a pet that will give you eggs from time to time, then the recommended breeds would be different.

I have listed a few most common and easy to raise breeds for beginners with varying needs. This is by no means a complete list but it will give you an idea of some great breeds to get you started.

Bantam-Cochin

This is a great breed for beginners. The hens are small in size and the most common color is black. However white, brown, red and golden laced are also recognized colors. They are sweet and adorable creatures. If you plan to keep hens for eggs, then bantam-cochins would be your best bet. They are calm and have easy going docile personalities. They adapt to a new environment fairly easily and are easy to tame. A bantam-cochin lays about one egg per day however exact count can vary according to the conditions.

If you're seeking a low maintenance, egg laying breed, then Bantam-Cochin would be perfect for you.

Delaware

These beautiful white-feathered creatures are also great for eggs. Their eggs are comparatively larger in size and lighter in color. If you want adorable, amusing pets as well as egg layers then you will love a Delaware. They are very keen and quick learners. They are also quite intelligent. Due to that they are also highly curious by nature and will fully explore your backyard and the surrounding area if you allow them to free range. Because of their smarter personalities, you'll have to let them out of the coop for at least two hours a day so that they can roam around and have fun. Like any intelligent pet, a Delaware will follow your lead and keep you company.

Dorking

If you're looking to breed your flock, then Dorkings will be perfect. They mate easily and without any hesitation. This might seem like an odd thing to say but some breeds are more reserved regarding their mating activities. Not this breed though. They also gain weight quickly and are perfect if you're looking for a breed to provide you with meat from time to time. They are not exceptionally good layers. However their delicious meat and the ability to reproduce quickly makes them ideal as a source for protein.

California Grey

This is another very interesting and friendly breed. They are highly intelligent and make great pets. Some owners report that their California Greys respond to the sound of their voices. This breed is an average to good layer and lays large white eggs which some people might prefer. California Greys are also prone to taking flight; however this tendency is not as bad as some other breeds. Though you'd still have to be vigilant when you let them out to free range.

Australorp

This is another breed of great layers. Australorp is one of those rare breeds that consistently lay good quality eggs regardless of the weather. In addition to that they are absolutely beautiful to look at. They are black with a slight metallic green sheen to their feathers. They look lovely roaming around the backyard. On top of that, they are also extremely friendly and responsive towards humans. They recognize their master and often approach him/her to get petted- almost just like a dog. They do not run in fright and neither do they fly, hence they make great pets.

Faverolles

This is another breed of laid back and easy going chickens. They do extremely well in captivity. So if you're someone who cannot allow the chickens to get out of their coop for a variety of reasons, then Faverolles are the breed you need. They are not much of a meat breed but lay consistent large, brown colored eggs. If you plan on keeping a rooster, then Faverolle roosters are comparatively less noisy and more friendly than the males of other breeds.

Rhode Island Red

This is the breed that comes to mind when you think of chickens. These are extremely common and easy to find. Rhode Island Reds are sort of like the best of both worlds. They gain enough weight to be used as meat birds but are also reasonable good layers. If you're undecided or need both eggs and meat then get a flock of Rhode Island Reds. They are easy to care for as they are much tougher than other fancy breeds. You can also find them at a reasonable price as most suppliers and breeders have them.

CROSS BREEDS

In comparison, cross breeds are better and more consistent layers than heritage breeds. Cross breeds are also cheaper to obtain. Brown Sex Links, Golden Comets and Cinnamon Queens are all cross breeds that are known for their exceptional laying capabilities.

Living Conditions of Your Chickens

Building a coop is not enough. You need to ensure that the living conditions and environment provided to your chickens are ideal and as close to nature as possible.

As a first step, you should ensure that the coop you are building is on soil or grass and not on any hard surface. The floor of your coop should not be lined with wood but should rest on your lawn. This is important because of two major reasons.

The first one being that dropping of your hens will not mix and degenerate naturally on a hard floor. It will create a mess that will smell horrible and will look awful. Also if your hens are living in that constrained area, they will constantly step over their own droppings. Just try to imagine how disgusting that would be. On the other hand, if there is soil and earth underneath, the droppings will mix with the soil and become compost. There will be less smell and mess.

The second reason is that hens enjoy eating worms and weeds from the soil. If you replace it with a hard floor, you will be denying your hens this natural source of food. They will survive on food that you give them but they'll stay happier if you allow them to scavenge as well.

Even if the floor of the coop is unlined, you'll still need to clean it at least on a monthly basis. There will be stray feathers and droppings all over the place. Chickens are very messy by nature. If you do not clean the area on a regular basis, it will start to smell. Since the coop will be so close to your house, it will waft in to your living area as well. Obviously you don't want that.

Generally once a month cleaning is enough. However if you have a large numbers of hens, biweekly cleaning might be required.

Chickens like many other animals and birds take dirt baths. No matter how muddy or dirty they look, do not wash them! Unlike parrots, chickens do not appreciate or enjoy a water spray. This could be fatal to them. Even for some undeniable need you do need to wash them, dry them with a blow dryer immediately afterwards.

Chickens have a habit of toppling over their eating and drinking containers. If you allow them to do it, they'll be constantly making a mess and wasting food. I recommend attaching the feeding tray to the side of your chicken coop. Alternatively you can also use a heavier container as their feeding tray. However this can be dangerous if by some mischief they topple it over themselves.

For severe winter months, simply insulating the coop will not do the trick. You will have to find some way to keep the coop heated. Generally a yellow light source works well. This has the added benefit of tricking your chickens believing that it is still day so that they'll lay more eggs. This is useful for the time of the year when days are very short. Or if you live in an area where it remains overcast.

However do not use stark white or bluish light as it will not produce the desired results.

No matter how well made, ventilated and comfortable the coop is, you chickens will still need to stretch their legs and feathers. Staying in captivity might depress your chickens which will as a result effect their health and laying capacity. Hence it is highly recommended that you let the out to roam around, even if it is for a short time.

When you take the decision to raise backyard chickens, you should also vow to keep them as healthy and as happy as possible. Taking care of their living conditions will ensure that your chickens are in their prime state.

Feeding Your Chickens

Beginners are often confused about how much food to feed their chickens. There is no hard and fast rule or equation that has been developed. It all depends on upon the breed, size, variety and lifestyle of your chickens. Generally speaking, meat varieties need more food than their egg laying counterparts as they need to put on weight. On an average, a regular hen needs about 1/4th of a pound of feed every day.

If you allow your chicken to free range then they will get some portion of their daily diet by eating insects, seeds and weeds. However if you keep them confined within the coop they'll need comparatively more food. On the other hand the chickens who stay within the coop are not burning as much calories, since they are not moving around that much, hence their food would need to be adjusted accordingly.

Chickens, especially the laying varieties, need a high amount of protein, calcium and grit in their daily diets. To maintain a good laying schedule, you'll need to incorporate enough protein in the diet. This protein can come from commercial feed that has a ratio of about 18-20% protein. Alternatively you can also feed them protein from external sources such as lentils.

Some owners raise their flock on a diet that consists primarily of corn. I firmly advise against it. Though corn is a great energy booster, it is still mainly carbohydrates and will not fulfill the dietary needs of your birds. Use corn as a supplement and not as the main part of your chicken's diet.

The commercial feed available in almost all pet stores comes in different varieties. The ratio of various components in the feed varies according to the type of the bird. Feed aimed at meat birds contains about 24% protein content. While the feed designated for laying hens contains about 18% protein and an ample amount of calcium and other minerals as well. Layer pellets are also available that are specifically designed for laying hens.

If I have not already mentioned enough advantages of keeping backyard chickens, then here's another one. Keeping chickens will prevent wastage of food.

Yes you read it right.

Your flock of chicken can eat about anything that you can eat. So if there are any leftovers from your table, you can easily give them to your chickens. Bonus points if the leftovers contain whole grains and vegetables. You can feed your chickens leftover boiled rice, vegetables and even vegetable stock. From your pantry, you can give your hens peanuts and different fruits as treats.

Just like humans, chickens also have varying tastes in food. You'll see that some of your birds really enjoy bananas while others are more partial to pumpkins. You can also give your flock leafy greens such as cabbage and spinach which are an excellent source of iron.

Some owners also report that they feed their chickens cooked scrambled eggs. I can imagine you raising your eyebrows right now. However let me explain. Eggs themselves are a very rich source of protein hence can work wonders for your undernourished chickens. If you are going to feed them eggs, then make sure to always cook them before feeding. If you give your hens raw eggs, then they'll start cracking the eggs they lay.

Though chickens can eat almost anything that is fit for human consumption, there are still a few exceptions. The primary one being dairy products. You should by no means feed your chicken cheese, butter, ice-cream or raw milk. The digestive system of chickens is unable to produce the enzyme lactose which is needed to digest milk and its derivatives.

You should also not give your chickens potato peels or onions as they contain solanine and thiosulphate respectively. Both of these chemicals are toxic to birds if ingested in high quantities. High quantities is the key here but I choose to play it safe and not give them any potato peels or onions.

Avocado is another fruit that some people advise against including in chicken feed. However there is not set consensus or scientific research to prove the harmfulness of avocado.

In nature, chickens eat all the time. You can call them greedy or just extremely fond of food. If left to their own devices, they'll eat all day long. You can either go with this flow and keep their feeding trays filled at all times or alternatively you can feed them at specific times. For convenience, most people feed their flock twice a day. Once in the morning and the other in the evening.

If you chose to go with the former option then ensure that the food tray doesn't attract pests such as rats. They can badly injure your birds.

If you can manage it, we recommend that you keep feeding trays full at all times. This is more natural for hens. They do not fill their little stomachs in one go but rather eat small portions over the course of the day. Either that, or you can allow them to free range and hunt some part of their food themselves.

Finding a workable feeding schedule and menu for your chickens is the work of trial and error. Just keep experimenting within the range of acceptable foods and you'll be able to work out a formula that both you and your chickens are satisfied with.

Health Concerns

Over the course of your experience, no matter how careful you are or how sanitary your conditions are, one or more of your chickens will fall ill. It is inevitable as they can get sick from so many different reasons. Most of the conditions that inflict backyard chickens are fortunately treatable. However it is still recommended that you should keep the contact number of your local avian vet in your address book in case of any emergency or advice that you might need.

For your convenience, I have compiled a list of most common inflictions and their recommended treatments.

Pests

This is one of the biggest nuisances to your chicken flock. Pests such as ticks, mites and fleas can prevail due to unsanitary living conditions. These pests latch themselves onto the birds and suck their blood. Though they can weaken the chicken, they are not highly dangerous. Most often common pests can be eliminated and prevented by improving sanitary conditions or a light spray of insecticide. Regular monthly cleaning of the coop will keep this problem at bay. If you allow your chickens to take dirt baths, they'll keep themselves clean and hence the pests will not have a chance to find thriving living conditions.

More dangerous parasites affect the respiratory and digestive systems of the bird. Most prevalent amongst parasitic diseases is "Coccidiosis" which affects the bird's digestive system. The first symptoms include blood in droppings, diarrhea and weight loss. If you notice any of these conditions, then take your pet to the vet immediately and have him/her prescribe a medicine. Hopefully your bird will recover in no time.

Another danger is from tapeworms and roundworms. This condition is extremely common in free range hens and is characterized by watery droppings and diarrhea. Tapeworms travel by the way of droppings and feces. Hence one bird can pass the parasite to all the others in the flock. It is recommended that you should isolate the affected hen as soon as you notice the symptoms. Then take your bird to a registered vet and follow his/her guidelines.

RODENTS

This is another very common problem, especially if you live in the suburbs or near the countryside. If you plan to feed your chickens by allowing them access to food at all times then rodents might pose a threat. The food and grains lying unattended might attract them for a feast. Not only will they considerably deplete you inventory by eating large amounts but they can also harm and even kill small chicks and sometimes adult chickens also. They might also attack your food store and inventory. Use traps and different available poisons to eliminate this danger. Just make sure your chickens don't have access to these traps or poisons.

EGG BINDING

This problem is exclusive to laying hens only. An egg of an exceptionally large size can become stuck inside the hen's vent. Despite the hen's efforts and force, it will not come out. The condition can cause immense pain and discomfort to your hen. However fortunately it is easily managed. If you notice that your hen is in pain or discomfort, then gently hold her and lubricate your finger with oil or any other suitable lubricant. Now insert your finger into her vent and with the other and gently massage the area between her feet. You would be able to feel the egg. With gentle pressure, ease it out of the vent and your hen would be good to go.

If you lack the confidence, you can also ask a veterinary student or a veteran chicken raiser to help you out.

Prolapse

This is another egg laying related problem. The pink insides of the hen's vent can hang outside after she has laid a large egg. There might even be some scabbing. The issue is easily solved by pushing the protruding part back by applying gentle pressure with your finger. Apply an ointment to the area afterwards to prevent risk of infection.

These four are the most common problems that your chickens can encounter. For detailed knowledge, I suggest reading a book dedicated specifically to poultry health.

Hatching Chicks

Breeding your flock and raising your own chicks can be beneficial in the long run if you plan to use your chickens for meat. Even if you do not intend to sacrifice your hens, you can still hatch chicks for the amazing experience that it offers. Chicks are extremely endearing and cute and it is a treat to see them around your backyard. Keep in mind that you will need a rooster for the breeding process.

Natural Hatching

The best way to hatch chicks is by allowing a hen to complete her clutch (a clutch typically contains around twelve eggs) and then letting her brood. Not only are the chicks hatched as healthy as they can possibly be but they also learn vital life lessons from their mother during their early life. Plus it is an absolute delight to watch little fluffs of feather trot after their mother and nestle in her feathers. There are very few sights as sweet, cute and complete as that.

If you plan to hatch chicks via the natural method then you'll have to select a mother and a suitable brooding place for her. Very often she'll brood in the same place where she nests. Hens can become very moody and possessive of their space when they are brooding. Hence it is recommended that you should isolate her so that she is not disturbed.

Once her clutch of around twelve eggs is complete, the hen will sit on them with her feathers spread out to keep the eggs warm and moist. During this time she'll peck at anyone who tries to approach her. The brooding period lasts for about twenty-one days. However it can vary from breed to breed. For these twenty-one days, the hen will leave its eggs only once a day to feed, drink and excrete. After the incubation period, all eggs will hatch around the same time.

When the eggs hatch, the hen will leave its brooding place for the first time in twenty-one days with all her little ones trotting behind her to get their first glimpse of the world. You need to have a swallow basin of water and some food available for the chicks around this time as they'll need to feed.

If you opt for the natural hatching method, there is not much that you can do apart from waiting. Make sure to not disturb the hen while she is brooding. Don't even try to take a look at her eggs or prod them during this time. Just have patience and let Mother Nature do its part.

Artificial Hatching

Natural hatching is great but it also has one major disadvantage. While the hen is brooding she will not lay anymore eggs. Therefore your total egg production will decrease. If you are worried about this and need the egg production, then you can hatch the chicks by placing them in an incubator.

There are many kind of incubators available on the market today. They come in varying designs and at different price points. Before you purchase the incubator, you need to think about these three factors.

1. How big of an incubator do you need?
2. Make sure the temperature is adjustable.

3. I prefer one with an adjustable humidity setting.

Many people also opt for temporary, homemade incubators but they do not yield very good results as two vital factors-temperature and humidity cannot be controlled.

Before you put the eggs in the incubator, I recommend running your incubator for about twenty-four hours and observe if the temperature and humidity remain within the recommended ranges. If there's too much variation than the incubator is faulty. Ideal temperature should be between 99-102oF while humidity should remain between 50-55%. The moisture is provided by a tray of water kept inside the incubator.

A fertilized egg is an alive being. It is breathing oxygen and giving out carbon dioxide. To promote adequate exchange of gases, there should be enough ventilation within the incubator. This is usually achieved by adjustable flaps on either side of the incubator itself.

Once the incubator is fully functional, it is ready to accept eggs. For your first batch, do not use the eggs of a very expensive breed. Also test your incubator on its first run by placing only a few eggs. Position the eggs with the wide end downwards in an aligned position. Avoid shaking the egg as it can disrupt the delicate balance.

Once you have placed them, turn the eggs every day. If this seems like a tedious process, you can buy incubators that turn the eggs automatically. When the incubation period is coming to an end, the humidity should be peaked up to 65%. During the last three days, avoid touching or turning the eggs.

When the chicks hatch, they have enough yolk in their bodies to sustain them for about 48 hours. Hence you do not need to make feeding arrangements right away. Freshly hatched chicks will be moist. Do not disturb them by attempting to dry them. They will dry due to the heat and fluff up by themselves. You can then shift them to a brooder.

Even the most accomplished of hatcheries have a success rate of about 50-75%. Not all eggs are fertilized and out of the fertilized ones, not all will hatch. Do not be dismayed if only a few eggs out of the clutch hatch. It is completely normal.

How To Take Care of a Chick

Whether you obtained your chicks from the pet store or you hatched eggs in an incubator, you'll need to familiarize yourself with their care. These little balls of fluff are gentle and fragile; therefore, they need more active care in comparison to their adult counter parts. If the eggs were hatched via natural hatching then there's nothing that you need to do. The mommy hen will take care of her babies.

If you hatched the eggs in an incubator, then by no means place the new born chicks in the coop with other adult chickens. They will peck on them and might even kill them. Instead prepare an appropriate brooder before the hatching. Just like the incubator was designed to ensure optimum conditions for the eggs, a box known as brooder should be set up to accommodate chicks.

Your brooder does not need to be fancy but should be functional. Any cardboard box, wooden box or even a dog pen can be turned into a brooder. All that you need is adequate space, lining and a heat source. Whatever box you select, make sure that it has enough ventilation. If the box is fully closed then drill or poke holes in its sides to promote an exchange of air. Chicks are very much active living beings and they need a constant supply of fresh air.

The brooder needs to be large enough that the chicks are able to move around and navigate easily. On an average, one chick needs to have about 1 sq. foot of space. As they grow up and increase in size, they'll need more space accordingly.

On the top of your selected box, hang a 250 Watts red bulb. This will act as a heat source. Do not use a bluish white bulb. When chicks are young, they naturally huddle close to their mother for warmth. However when you are raising them, you need to provide a separate heat source. Many new owners make the mistake of not keeping the chicks warm and the poor souls die as a result.

Your bulb should ideally be hanging at about eighteen inches from the floor of the brooder. However it should be adjusted according to the weather. I recommend fixing your heat source so it can easily be altered up and down.

You'll also need to line the floor of the brooder. Chicks poop a lot. They virtually excrete all the time. So the lining material should be something absorbent. To prevent it from getting smelly, you'll need to change it often.

Wood shavings are the safest choice as a lining material. By no means use straw or hay. It can irritate the respiratory tract of the chicks. Do not line the box with newspaper either as it is slippery. The lining needs to be something that is firm and the feet of the chicks can hold onto it. Very much like real earth. Otherwise they will not be able to retain their grip and it will result in splayed feet. Splayed feet is a condition in which the feet of the chicks point in opposite directions which make it impossible for them to walk.

You also need to keep a ready source of food and water available at all times. For small chicks, there is a starter feed available on the market. This is high in protein which is essential for development. The particle size of starter feed is smaller than regular feed which makes it more suitable for little chicks. As they grow up, you'll also need to provide them with grit to aid digestion. Grit in their stomachs helps to break down food into smaller pieces to aid digestion. I recommend that instead of placing food in their feeding tray, you should scatter it on the floor of the brooder occasionally. This way the chicks will learn to look for their food instead of eating from a singular source.

Young chicks need loads of water. A lot of chicks die at a young age due to thirst and dehydration. Always have a swallow tray of water in the brooder. Make sure that the water basin are not too deep or there can be a risk of chicks drowning in it. I recommend an actual chick waterer as the safest and easiest to use watering dish. However, you can also use a shallow tray with pebbles in it. I recommend mixing necessary vitamins and mineral supplements in the water to aid chick growth.

For the first four weeks, it is recommended you keep the brooder inside the house. The inside of the house is warm and there is less chance of weather affecting the health of the chicks. Outside, uncanny predators such as hawks and rodents can attempt to attack the chicks and scare them in the process.

When you first introduce chicks into the brooder, dip their beak into the water basin before letting them in. This way they'll know where to find water. For the first few days, you can also feed them sweet water. This will give them an instant boost of energy. This is highly recommended if your chicks have travelled in the process of getting to you.

Almost daily, you should watch your chicks carefully for signs of anything that might seem off. Inspect the rear end of each chick for a phenomenon known as "pasting up". This is characterized by poop drying up and blocking the chick's vent. If left untreated, it can be fatal. Fortunately the remedy is quite simple. Just take a wash cloth and dip it in warm water and with gentle rubbing motions clear the area.

Sometimes for some chicks, the placenta (black string like structure) might still be sticking to their rear ends. Do not pull or tug at it. This can lead to an injury. Instead let the chick be and it will fall off by itself within a few days.

You should also observe the social behavior of your flock and see if everyone is eating alright. If one chick is secluded or if others are ganging up on it and pecking it, then isolate it and feed this chick separately.

Always keep a look out for telltale signs such as the chicks huddling together or making alot of noise. In most cases, it means that they are feeling cold. Adjust their heat source accordingly.

If you intend to raise your chicks as pets then get them used to handling. Hold them, stroke them and pet them so that they get accustomed to being touched. If you do it from a young age, your chickens will grow up fearless and loving towards humans. I recommend you always wash your hands before and after touching your birds to help prevent illness.

As time passes and your chicks grow up, their needs will evolve. After about eight weeks you can shift from starter feed to growing feed and start feeding them natural items as well. As they increase in size, they will need more space and might not fit in the brooder any longer. It might be the time to relocate them.

PECKING ORDER

Chickens are social birds and do not like to live alone. This is in stark contrast to the behavior of some other birds such as parrots, which can manage quite well on their own. Hence it is a bad idea to keep only one hen. There should at least be two to keep each other company.

Within a flock of chickens exists a pecking order. It is just part of their social structure. Pecking order is formed right after birth and is very difficult to change. This makes it difficult to merge new birds with the existing flock. The introduction of a new bird disrupts the social structure as the chickens do not know where the new member stands within the pecking order.

The alpha member of the pecking order has the rights to all the necessities and luxuries first. It is usually a male rooster but an old and particularly aggressive hen can also hold the alpha position. After the alpha, there is a neatly defined order all the down to the last and the weakest member. Every member higher in order can bully and peck on the members lower in order. Such that everyone can bully the lowest member while the one on the second number will only be bullied by the alpha but will freely peck on everyone else.

The alpha member has the first right to food, water and comfort. He/She gets to eat and drink before everyone else. A hen of higher order will drive away the other hens from her choice nesting place by pecking on them. If the alpha member is a male then he holds the first mating right with the hens of the flock. No other cockerel can approach them in his presence.

If the alpha becomes wounded, weak or dies then the second in command will take its place. This is the only way that the pecking order can evolve.

Just keep this in mind if you plan on introducing new members to the flock. However a somewhat successful method is to keep the new members and the old flock separated by a screen so that they can see each other but not inflict any harm. Hopefully with some time, they will get used to each other and work out a suitable pecking order.

The system of a pecking order might sound cruel but this is the chickens' way of maintaining order within the flock. There is nothing that you can do to change it. If you plan on keeping backyard chickens then you should come to terms with it.

Dealing with Predators

A flock of chickens can attract all sorts of predators looking for a quick meal. It can be heart breaking to lose your chickens to a wild animal or bird. Your flock is more prone to attack if it free ranges or has small chicks in the midst.

Most animals are on the lookout for food during the day. So that is the most dangerous time. However that does not make the dark time entirely safe. Wild cats can also attack your birds during the night.

The most common predators are wild cats, stray dogs, hawks, and crows. If you live near an area of wilderness than other animals might also show up. You need to prepare differently for aerial and earth bound attackers.

The first and foremost precaution that you should take is to ensure that the mesh of the coop is strong enough to hold against a vigorous attack by sharp claws and teeth. No matter how strong, the mesh will only hold for a few minutes. The claws of cats and the teeth of the dogs are razor sharp and can tear at the mesh quickly. Ideally, solid iron rods are recommended instead of net mesh. However it might be quite pricy. If your coop has a wire mesh, then make sure that it is accessible to you even in the middle of the night. So that if you hear any commotion, you can rush out to rescue your chickens.

A wire mesh will generally keep out air borne predators such as hawks and eagles. Your chickens are more prone to danger from them if you allow them to free range. Birds of the Accipitridae family have spectacular sight and amazing diving abilities. They can descend from the sky at bolting speed, snatch a bird and then fly back again. Full grown chickens are too heavy for the birds of prey to carry. However they can easily grab hold of chicks. The mother will try to protect her chick but she is no match against the might of a predator of that much power. If there are chicks in the flock, then it is ideal if you only allow them to free range in your presence. Once the chicks grow up, it will be much safer.

Another shrewd, clever and often ignored predator is the black crow. It will not attack your chickens but will make a snack out of the eggs. Crows can break eggs with their long beaks and sip the eggs like a drink. The best way to prevent this loss is to ensure that your hens lay inside the coop in their designated nesting places. However some crows are so cunning that they can even find their way inside the coop. You can rely on a scare crow but most crows now-a-days take no notice of it. The only sure shot way is to make it a habit to remove the eggs the first thing in the morning to beat the crow in the race to get the egg first.

You can also build a high fence around your backyard to keep out stray cats and dogs. However if the fence is low, the cats and dogs might jump over it to get into your backyard. Only a fence of considerable height will effectively keep them out. Installing a high fence will cost a lot but will be very safe for your birds.

Another solution to the problem of predators is to adopt a canine friend for your flock of chickens. A well bred and intelligent dog will guard your flock, keep off the predators and will of course be your best friend. However, a dog is a high maintenance pet and you should only get one if you can provide it with care, discipline and affection. A misbehaved dog can do more damage to your flock than good.

Some breeds such as Bernese Mountain Dogs and Great Danes are more bird friendly than others. Shepherd breeds such as a Border Collie are also amazing and take their job as a guard for your flock very seriously.

When you make the decision of raising backyard chickens , it is your responsibility to ensure their safety. Do not take it lightly. Make the appropriate arrangements so that both you and your birds are content and safe.

Conclusion

I sincerely hope that you found this book helpful in your quest of gaining knowledge about keeping backyard chickens. Raising backyard chickens is a healthy and fun activity with many rewarding benefits such as delicious eggs and meat.

Your backyard chickens can also be a great educational experience for the kids in your family. They can learn about sustained living and responsibility through them. It will help them to grow up to be animal loving individuals.

If you end up with a surplus of eggs and you cannot use all of them, they also make excellent gifts for friends, neighbors and relatives. You can even turn it into a small scale business by selling the extra eggs. The demand and price for organic eggs is quite high so it can be very profitable.

If you have finally decided to keep backyard chicken then I applaud your decision and wish you all the best in your endeavors. May your flock of chickens be a source of delight to you and your family.

Please Leave a Review

Finally if you enjoyed this book, please leave a review. This will help other people to find it and enjoy the wonderful joy that backyard chickens bring. You can leave a review by following this link: BackyardProducer.com/go/Backyard-Chickens-Review or by following this link https://www.amazon.com/review/create-review?ie=UTF8&asin=B00U1HDBDA&channel=detail-glance&nodeID=&ref_=dp_top_cm_cr_acr_wr_link#

Don't Forget Your Free Gift

If you haven't already downloaded your free chicken coop plans then do so now. It is totally free and will give your chickens a beautiful home. You can get that at BackyardProducer.com/chicken-coop-pdf

Printed in Great Britain
by Amazon